C000136968

The Collected Poems
Volume 2
2016-2020

Graham A. Rhodes.

First Edition
Templar Publishing, Scarborough 2020

First published 2020
Templar Publishing, Scarborough, England

Cover photograph –
Graham Rhodes, Aakschipper Images

Acknowledgements

Well this is the second volume of my collected works. and the acknowledgements are the same as the last one with a few additions. Some are friends, some acquaintances, and some I've never met, but over the years all of them have in some way influenced what you are about to read. It gets a bit long but when you are putting together a lifetimes worth of poetry there's a lot to acknowledge. So here we go, with love and thanks to -

Dave Pruckner (Check out his book and buy it!), Tommy Simpson, Nick Jones, Gordon Davison, Ian & Stuart Pearson, Phil Finch, Kev & Bonk, Andi Lee, John Cooper Clarke, Mike Hardin, John Middleton, Roy Webber & Wally, Kinky Friedman, Paul Simon, Roger McGough, Ogden Nash, Roy Harper, Seahouse, Velma, Captain Beefheart, Frank Zappa, Randy California, John Stewart, Thomas Pynchon, Eric Gill, Alan Garner, Gary Barrett (& Life Support & Stone Cold Sober), Bandanna, Will Hay, Aldo & His Orphans, Fibbers, Martin, Nigel & Wayne,(Hardliners all), Vivian Stanshill, Compton Mackenzie, Dylan Thomas, Groucho Marx, Max Miller, Ian Dury, Billy Bennett, Marriott Edgar, Bob Williamson, John Otway, Tim Minchin, Peter Tinniswood, Raymond E. Feist, David Eddings, Terry Pratchett, Bill Hicks, Denis Leary, Sister Gregory, Madge & Lawrence Rhodes, Samantha Rhodes, Jesse Hutchinson, The Baytown Rattlers, Eli & The Blues Prophets, Toby Jepson, Yvonne, Ross Dransfield, The Merchant and all who drink in her. Simon, Captain Ants & The Jawline crew, Nils Arnold & Northern Riots (Luke, Kris & Brad) Mr. Jim & Indigo Alley, Crooners

Open Mic at The Wapentake, Frankie & Heather (& Granddad), Chris, Dave MacGregor & Coast & County Radio, Julia Wray (lodger extraordinaire and emergency cat sitter), The Badgers Of Bohemia, Tubbs & Missy, Anna Shannon, John Watton & all at The Cellars (the place to be seen), Joe Solo, the "We Shall Overcome" team & finally Ysanne in the hope that one day it will turn up in her bookshop.

Introduction

In the summer of 2019 I was 70 and I'm still going! Since my first book of poetry emerged I have gigged all over the place, and found myself writing new material both to keep the act refreshed and current but also because the last few years have been bloody crazy, both personally and in the outer world, of politics and various other events that I felt a need to comment on. Hence the last few years have been some of the most creative I've encountered and all the poems in here are a result of my reaction to that craziness. Since the last book and since the Covid19pandemic attack of 2020 I've also made great use of the internet, doing live and pre-recorded gigs and putting everything up on YouTube and my Facebook Performance Poet web site.

Many of these poems are the ones I perform Others have never been performed, but still deserve to see the light of day. Some may cause raised eyebrows, some might even cause offence. If so I do not apologise. Hopefully they'll make people think, many are intended to shock and to get a reaction in the hope that someone, somewhere can do something to halt the injustice, the inequality the and get off their arses and do something about the state of British politics. I hope you enjoy them.

Graham Rhodes
Scarborough 2020.

The Collected Poems
2016 - 2020

I always start my live set off with this poem. It's a sort of shock and awe approach to my performance and tends shuts up any talkers. It also sets the tone for what's to come.

This Poem is Shit

You can be shit faced
Have shit for brains
Shit or get off the pot

Smoke shit
Talk shit
Or even be shit hot

You can throw shit
Give a shit
Or duck when it hits the fan

You can be in deep shit
Tough shit
When everything turns wrong

You can look like shit
Feel shit
Go like shit off a shovel

Find yourself
up shit creek
without any paddle

Have a shower of shit
Get your shit together
Bears shit in the woods
cos its always shitty weather

There's heavy shit
Weird shit….

But please, don't be offended
This is just a shitty poem
I'm just fucking glad its ended.

Sometimes poems just happen, words form without any explanation or reason. This is one of them. Never performed.

The Strider

The Strider
walk's the hilltops

The Walker
stride's the Dales

The Stalker
walk's the forest paths
and haunts the midnight trails

The Merchant
goes to market

The Riders
cross the fen

The Pilgrim
walks behind the cross
avoids the road to Hell

The Gambler
plays his money

The Winner
take's it all

The Priest
answers the mystery
by saying there is no mystery at all.

This was written after seeing the 1953 Marlon Brando movie "The Wild One", that also introduced me to Lee Marvin.

Stance
Like a black rebel motorcyclist
roaring through the night
like a man dressed up a white sheet
hoping to cause a fright
once it's been kick started
you can never stop the dance
you've got to keep your attitude
got to maintain your stance
you've got to keep the game alive
follow the bouncing ball
make sure you keep on keeping on
when your back's against the wall
if you go down, go down fighting
you'll not win if you're not in the game
never settle for mediocrity
nobody is the same
never turn the other cheek
just tighten up your belt
the meek shall inherit the earth
only if it's OK with everyone else.

The year 2020 will always be remembered for the year Covid-19 struck. As I write this we are still in the midst of lockdown. This is an observation from that lockdown.

Jogging Pants

They've been the longest weeks
in the history of ever
stuck inside our houses
irrespective of the weather
just bit players
in this game of life
sitting out the lock-in
avoiding all the strife
panning for gold
in the YouTube channels
scraping stuff to watch
from the bottom of a barrel
it's become our entertainment
that's how we spend our nights.
no one's had a haircut
we all look like a fright
all we've worn is jogging pants
for the last three months
and turned our communications
into a set of grunts
thank God for the Internet
Face Time, Zoom and others

keeping the connection between
sister, brothers, mothers
not going out to shop
having everything delivered
all this home drinking is
messing with my liver
watching wild life take over the street
going for a walk
and just the badgers that you meet
we're all hand washing but
it's the world that's getting clean
all on account of that Covid19

This is my reaction to a very real and ineffectual
Governmental approach to the Corvid-19 epidemic.
History will judge them and us.

You don't....
You don't send a painter
off to work without a brush
you don't send a driver
a load without a truck
you don't send a soldier
to war without a gun
any mathematician can work it out
using just a couple of sums
you don't find a banker
without their stocks and shares
you don't find a vicar
without a bible and a prayer
you don't find a forest
without a fallen tree
you can't fight a crisis
without a cup of tea
you don't find the Telegraph
criticising any Tories
you can't find a boxer
that can knock out Tyson Fury
but you do expect a health trust
to look after all its workers
and wish that our Government
were not penny pinching shirkers.

Another poem from the Covid-19 epidemic and the lockdown period of 2020.

It won't be all right

It'll be alright in the morning
but it's right fucked up in the night
it'll seem like a storm in a teacup
but right now it's a bloody fright

It'll all come out in the wash they say
even though the bed-sheets are stained
every cloud has a silver lining
when outside it's pissing with rain

Always look on the bright side
but what if both sides are dark?
always try the hair of the dog
but it's bite is worse than its bark

There's no such thing as a safe haircut
once cut you can't put it back
and nothing writhes and wriggles like
two ferrets in a sack

each Thursday night the voters go out
to express their applause of shame
why they voted to hack and cut
all in austerities name

As the triumphant Daily Torygraph
vomits right wing crap
machine gunners of class warfare
the PM's back they slap

For God's sake open up your eyes
look around and linger
when all the rhetoric has been and gone
you'll know where to point the finger.

Yet another poem from the Covid-19 epidemic. This one is in reaction to all the conspiracy theories that littered the internet.

Strange Days
(Even the conspiracy theory is a conspiracy)
Strange days
unusual connections
strange voices
echoing reflections
of card sharks
and wheeler dealers
snake oil salesmen
crooked faith healers
you tube prophets
conspiracy theorists
ridiculing science
ignoring the realists
so many experts
so many opinions
so many big brains
treating us like minions
patronising, talking down
so instead of wearing smiles
we can only wear a frown
it ain't very good
for our mental health
so please keep your opinions
to yourself.

Another poem from the Covid-19 epidemic, and my anger at a Government that seemed so unprepared and so arrogant in their reactions to the approaching disaster.

For the 2020 Tory Government
One day there'll be a reckoning
one day we'll mark their cards
one day we'll ask them questions
why they made our life so hard
why they dropped the safety net
why they short changed us
why they sold us down the river
and chucked the NHS beneath a bus
why they ignored warnings
from experts in their field
in order to maximise profits
give shareholders a bigger yield
to appease their drooling followers
who read the Telegraph and the Mail
how come we have a government
who started out to fail
 why they've lied to voters
to make themselves look good
now they've played their hands we see
their hands are drenched in blood
don't you dare clap for the nurses
that's just hypocrisy
when you all cheered to underpay them
you'll never represent me

And yet another poem written as a result of the Covid-19 lockdown and the 2020 epidemic, well what do you expect if you put a poet in lockdown.

Virus

I'm staying at home today
I'm staying at home tomorrow
I'm staying at home for the next four
months
I'm leaving the world in great sorrow

I suppose I could repaint the kitchen
I could write a new masterpiece
but it'll be four months of beer, Netflix and pizza
and I'll end up looking very obese

Perhaps I should buy myself jigsaws
or teach myself crochet or knitting
or get up and sort out the garden
not just look out the window just wishing

Perhaps I'll become alcoholic
but I never stocked up on the booze
and I can't go and scare myself shitless
cos there's no bog paper left in my loo

So I'll just sit here and scratch my own bollocks
and watch the grim news on TV
and try to stay safe and hoping the virus
doesn't come nowhere near me

And pity the poor sods who go out
and face this thing right face to face
the Government's treatment of workers
seems to me just a fucking disgrace

There's not enough gear for our nurses
no visors no mask or no gowns
no protection for them in our care homes
one sneeze and we all will fall down

Some countries have handled it badly
some countries have handled it worse
but our lot just dithered and dithered
and hoped that the thing would disperse

So one day when this thing blows over
for them that is gone raise your glass
look to Whitehall for some sort of reckoning
ask why they had their heads up their arse

This just had to be written and said

Dominic Cummings

Pinocchio just grew his nose
but this man's lies won a country
he made us all Little Englanders
hnd turned us all into Xenophobic's

He won the vote about Brexit
by painting lies on the side of a bus
he laughed all the way to the polling booth
and the ones who got ripped off were us

He thinks he's above the working class
his daddy owns a rich farm
the rest of us can all go to hell
as long as he comes to no harm

He sits at the highest table
and thinks rules are made to be broken
but when rules concern our life and death
the man has just got to be joking

Most Tories have gathered to save him
politicians disguised as human beings
but we know they cannot be trusted
Conservative twisted wheeling's and dealings

We know Cummings should be going
and wonder how he kept his position
and just what dirt he has over Boris
and can the Spectator send him to perdition

Confession was held in a garden
weasel words and never a sorry
a prick among roses, spinning a yarn
ahere the truth got chucked under a lorry

Cummings must know all the secrets
everything about Boris's sleaze
and that Boris will catch more than a virus
if Cummings ever chooses to sneeze

This is my promise to my friends and the world in general when we are eventually allowed to go outside and try to regain some semblance of normality.

When all this shit is over
When all this shit is over
we'll sit down inside a bar
we'll strap ourselves into our seats
and drink away the scars
the bruises and the broken bones
that life has dealt our way
and toast all of our enemies
come that wondrous drunken day
we'll throw the glasses to the floor
and curse our so called friends
we don't forgive, we don't forget
we'll never make amends.
When all this shit is over
we'll sit there face to face
we'll stumble round and mumble
about each other's saving grace
we'll show the world we matter
we'll show the world we care
we'll drink that bloody bar so dry
till we've drunk away our wear and tear
we'll drink till nighttimes over
we'll drink till break of day
we'll down the hatch and raise the roof
till they carry us away.

Like I said at the start of this book. I was 70 in 2019 and am very aware of getting old and the fun things old age brings us.

Time Goes by So Fast

Sometimes it's better not to remember
sometimes it's better to forget
sometimes it's better just to turn the page
and wipe away the debt
nostalgia ain't what it used to be
don't look back with sorrow
when all is finally said and done
today will be yesterday tomorrow
time is what you make it
it's never on your side
between the living and the dead
is where two worlds collide
so always live for tomorrow
and don't dwell in the past
cos when you're getting older
time goes by so fast
and one day they'll call you Spiderman
cos you can't get out of the bath.

I live in Scarborough, by the seaside, and whenever the sea fret comes in the foghorn starts up its mournful sound can be heard everywhere.

Mournful

There are some mournful sounds
that haunt our world
like a bloke bewailing
his long lost girl
a tom cat howling
right through the night
a boxer who's just
lost his fight
a gambler when his bet
goes down
children screaming
at the scary clown
an illegal parker
who's just got a ticket
a batsmen when the balls
hit his middle wicket
a banshee yelling
at the hunters moon
an aristocrat whose
lost their silver spoon

a magician when
the trick goes wrong
a singer when they
forget their song
a wrestler whose
had enough
a ghost hunter whose
learnt the truth
a virgin whose
in the family way
but saddest is a foghorn
on a foggy day

If you know me or have ever read anything about me, you'll know that back in the day I was a designer for bands like The Police & The Cramps and was backstage at the now legionary Victoria Park Gig at Hackney. This is poem about those heady punk days.

Punk Rocker

I saw The Police
I went to see the Clash
 bought all their albums
spent all of my cash

I saw the Rezillos
and Sham 69
going to punk gigs
took up all of my time

I saw the Pogues
when they were Pogue Malone
but I never got to see
a band called The Ramones

I saw Peter and
the Test Tube Babies
even had a pint with
old Rat Scabies

I saw Chelsea
and Alternative TV
all that speed was almost
the death of me

I saw Ian Dury
I went there on my own
but I never got to see
a band called The Ramones

I saw The Damned
and X-Ray Spex
I always held the Slits
in great respect

I saw the Pistols
and The Ruts as well
The Voidoids fronted
 by Richard Hell

I saw The Tubes
and lots of unknowns
But I never got to see
a band called The Ramones.

Yes I fear that over time and as a result of various rocky life events, I have developed into a grumpy old man and here's the proof..

Grumpy

I'm fed up with the football
and the wages players get
I'm fed up with all the adverts
telling me to place a bet

I'm fed up with the weather
I'm fed up with the news
the only music I listen to
is the bloody fed up blues

I'm fed up with the companies
that have run our railways down
I'm fed up with mobility scooters
that knock pedestrians down

I've had enough of Christmas
starting in July
I'm fed up with the lack of meat
inside a Birds Eye frozen pie

I'm fed up of fireworks
going off on every occasion
I'm fed up with politicians
practicing evasion

I'm fed up with everything
the world has turned to shit
but then I'm forced to the conclusion
I'm just a bloody grumpy git

Again a poem from my aged, warped perspective. I'm a great believer in Murphy's Law, you know it's the one the simply claims that "Sod was an optimist"!

Bite The Bullet

Sometimes it's better to bite the bullet
before the bullet bites you back
sometimes you've got to ride the wave
before it knocks you flat

When you tumble off the horse
you've just got to climb back on
and stop all the gambling
when the gambling stops being fun

Sometimes when you stand on the edge
it's better to jump off
if you don't need a shit or a shave
you better off with a cough

If the moving finger writes
what happened to all of the pens?
and where there's a will and a way
there's always relatives to offend

Always take the hair of the dog
although it's hit and miss
but it's better than the dare of the hog
especially if you're pissed

Always tread the righteous path
even if you swing to the left
always smile when you go to work
in case you get left on the shelf

Give it the best shot that you've got
beware the bourgeoisie
we've all been down so fucking long
it seems like up to me.

This was my response at receiving a bloody massive bill
from a solicitor for a job they originally agreed to do for
a flat fee. Hell have no fury like a poet having to pay 10
times more that he originally agreed to.

Deadly Creatures

Sharks are bloody vicious
with no expression in their eyes
Vultures will sit and wait
and watch you till you die

Poison spiders will weave their webs
and fill you full of venom
Piranhas will eat you up
not even leave a tendon

A rattlesnake will get you
if you ignore its rattle
A scorpion has a sting in the tail
and kills you with a cackle

A polar bear will stalk you
and tear you limb from limb
A jellyfish can kill you
when you're going for a swim

Alligators and crocodiles
will give you a nasty fright
The Brazilian Wandering Spider
will give you a deadly bite

But the deadliest creature of them all
a money and soul destroyer
is that blood sucking vampire
that calls himself a lawyer.

The internet is a minefield of false and misleading adverts and stuff that's just blatant lies. This is my comment on the matter.

Click Bait

Conspiracy theories
and downright lies
click bait stories
designed to cause surprise
like Hitler is alive and well
and living on the moon
and aliens have landed
in the mountains near Rangoon
Elvis Presley has a job
in a Butlin's holiday camp
and your willie is going to drop off
If it gets exposed to damp
Paul McCartney died
and was replaced by a double
and off screen Pepper Pig
is a trotter full of trouble
The Ancient Egyptians
were the cause of nine eleven
and all good children
when they die, will go to heaven

Click bait stories
a sack of bloody shite
don't be taken in
by a pack of whopping lies
lay the blame on Murdock
blame it on the Russians
blame the social media
for publishing such rubbish
Fakebook, Twatter
and other web site tools
making money from conspiracies
taking us for click bait fools

I love old sayings. This poem is just me having fun with them by mixing them all up and adding a few new ones.

Sayings

You can lead a horse to water
but a pencil has to be lead.
We'll burn that bridge when we get to it
is a phrase that's seldom said.
 He's not the smartest egg in the attic
is what everybody thinks.
And you can put your rubbish in another man's bin
but you can never make him drink.
I'll stand my ground and stake my claim
because hell hath no fury.
And I'll say what I want to say
until all the cows freeze over.
I'm never counting on my chickens
because that's not rocket science.
I've made my bed and I've watched it boil
just like another kitchen appliance.
My sleeping dog has woken up
and bitten my lazy hen.
And one man's meat is another man's fish
unless he counts to ten.

There's something afoot out there
and it's not just a twelve inch ruler.
And oranges aren't the only fruit
because cucumbers are cooler.
Never wash yourself in public
if your underpants are dirty.
And you can lead a horse to water
but it'll never win the two-thirty.

I celebrated the end of 2019 by falling over and breaking my hip. A huge thanks go out to the NHS and the staff of Leeds General Infirmary, and my daughter that put up with me living in her spare bedroom for eight weeks.

Dangerous Things

There's lots of danger
in the world today
global warming
lack of pay
bush fires burning
the climate turning
the seas are rising
the lack of housing
corporate greed
and people in need
mad men with hammers
Internet spammers
gangsters with guns
bears with buns
nuclear weapons
Armageddon beckons
old C.D.'s by Milley Cyrus
bats diseased with deadly virus
Piranha's in a swimming pool
scientists with their sliding rules

Hitler when he stopped painting houses
ex's and divorced spouses
the world is full of dangerous pricks
but the worse of all are old men with sticks

I like Pukka Pies, what else is there to say

Pukka Pies

Everything is bloody pukka
with a pukka Pukka pie
microwaves in just four minutes
guaranteed to satisfy

Tender bits of steak and gravy
all inside a shortcrust pie
every bit is as good as sex
Pukka pies make you wanna sigh

Far superior to those at Greggs
they leave Cooplands right behind
cos there's no bits and lips and gristle
inside a pukka Pukka pie

You can return your pizza delivery
chuck your Big Mac on the floor
shove your Whopper up your arse
it's pukka Pukka pies for evermore

Fish and chips are so mundane
with or without the mushy peas
a pukka pie is far more tasty
pukking guaranteed to please

Pukka Pies are our heritage
they've made pies since '63
The Peoples Pies have kept us going
since t'Beatles sang Please Please Me

The countries full of National Treasures
from Mr. Kipling to Stephen Fry
but there's nowt to beat those chips and gravy
and a pukka Pukka pie!

Thanks to Yvonne for the punch line to this, once I heard it I had to create a poem around it.

Phobias

I'm scared of beautiful women
I'm venustraphobic

I don't like spiders either
I'm also arachnophobia

I don't like the colour purple
i'm porphyrophobic

I'm not too fond of water
I guess I'm hydrophobic

I really don't like wriggly snakes
I must be ophidophobic

And I don't like things that are dead
I'm necro bloody phobic

I always wear zips I don't like buttons
I'm Koumpounophobic

I don't like clicking of the clock
I'm chronomentrophbic

I don't like things that are big
I'm megalophobic

I don't like things that are small
I'm must be micropohbic

I think I'm scared of my phobia
That means I'm phobophobic

And I'm really scared of giants
I guess I'm fe fi fo phobic.

Another poem that's really a whinge about getting old.

Everything is getting smaller

Everything is getting smaller
Cheesy Whatsits and Lion Bars
everything is getting smaller
apart from debt and working hours

Wagon Wheels and Tussocks Tea Cakes
portions in the take-aways
entitlements, and personal benefits
just blink once and they've gone away

Snickers Bars were a damn sight bigger
when they were called Marathons
Gummy Bears and Jelly Babies
one quick suck and then they're gone.

Everything is going up
and bugger all is coming down
despite the force of natural gravity
The British Pound has hit the ground.

Everything is getting smaller
we seem to suffer it all together
everything is getting smaller
especially mine in this cold weather

Another poem with a punch line. After surviving a heart attack in 2018 and breaking my hip in 2019 and being diabetic, I've taken more pills in these last few years than one can shake a stick at (should you wish to!).

Pills

There's lots of little pills today
to take your aches and pains away
the white ones make us better
yellow for go-getters
green ones stop the blow-up
one too many and you throw up
blue ones make it harder
and help that loving ardour
pink one help us sleep at night
green ones make us feel like shite
a purple one can make us smart
a black one just explodes the heart
a brown one helps you if you mourn
three too many and you grow horns
one pill makes you smaller
one pill makes up tall
but the ones that mother gives you
stops you climbing up the wall
there's pills to help you diet
pills to make you fat

pills to stop the aging
pills that make you chat
pills to make you happy
pills to make you sad
pills that turn you inside out
till you think you're going mad
pills that act like magic
you'll swear that you've been hexed
I got some Viagra to stop the brewers droop
and offered my old lady a night of super sex
I was so pissed off when she said she'd have the soup.

Although I'm computer literate I am worried about how much technology is taking over my life and has the ability to go wrong.

Technology

My X-Box's eloped with my Playstation Fourm
my intelligent fridge won't open up its door
my electronic kettle is spying on me
and my delivery drones got stuck in a tree
my TV remote switches on the heating
me pop up toaster is embedded in the ceiling
my laptop and tablet won't talk to each other
cos I don't know the maiden name of my mother
my cash card got eaten by the automatic bank
and my keep fits fucked cos my rowing machine sank
me food processer has starved to death
and my ioniser leaves me very short of breath
a passing vibrators just shot up the cats bum
my electronic toothbrush has ripped out all me gums
my Nicam digitals run amok
my vertical hold has come unstuck
can't remember where I put my memory stick
I'm in a digital world but my digit doesn't fit.

Despite the title of the book I found these next two poems from 1970 when they were printed in the second issue of the now legendary Krax Magazine

Snake Eyes

I remember she glided
towards me like a snake
and coiled her arms
around me
as she talked her tongue
flicked from side to side
I thought I was in control
but she held me hypnotized.
It was only later
when she shed her skin
I realised she never batted an eyelid.

Tracker Dogs

Tracker dogs
search the fields
where we made love
I sent them to search
in case any traces remained
now you're gone
you didn't even stay long enough
for the grass to straighten itself
it's all still flattened
where we lay together
in a field with tracker dogs

I've done a few gigs for Extinction Rebellion and wear their badge at gigs. I'm not the only one worried about the future of the planet.

The Waters Rising

The rain is bloody pissing down
the waters getting higher
I'm not too sure this is the time
to be a climate change denier

the Polar Bears are dying out
the Arctic's getting hotter
I set a mousetrap yesterday
and caught myself an otter

I need a pair of Long Johns
I need some warm mulled ales
I need some inside warming
outside is blowing up a gale

There's hurricanes in Virginia
tornadoes in the West
back here the winters getting colder
I need that thermal vest

But climate change is not a joke
despite what politicians say
because they all got shares in oil
they claim wind power will never pay

and that's the problem that we face
vested interests in t'corridors of power
they'll still be trading stocks and shares
as we face our final hour

As lowlands disappear beneath the sea
and waters rise above our heads
there'll be no one left to say "I told you!"
cos we'll all be bloody well dead.

I love puns, spoonerisms and twisting words around and
I this is one of the best I've come across in years.

I fell in love with a Vampirena

I fell in love with a Vampirena
it was love at first bite
she couldn't have been more obscener
we slept all day and made love all night
and when she went to McDonalds
she gave everyone a fright
she ordered her Big Mac uncooked and raw
and was offended that they don't do
bloody milk shakes any more
she hangs upside down
when she goes to sleep
I tried doing that
but I fell down in a heap
she loves red meat
but avoids having steaks
can't do her make up in a mirror
so she makes mistakes
she always drinks her soup
before its clotted
and drinks bloody marys
cos Mary's veins are carotid

every party we go to
someone tries to lay her
so she eats all the food
she's my hungry Vampire, the buffet slayer.

The dire consequence of eating wonky kebabs that, after a few pints, are God's gift to hunger, but half an hour after eating it you can't stand the damn thing anymore and you wonder why you thought eating it was a good idea. Somehow it turned into an ecological poem..

Wonky Kebab

It's all the fault of
that wonky kebab
the one that I bought
to add to the flab
after six pints of bitter
and shots made of glitter
that now seems to be blocking the loo

It's all the fault of
that wonky kebab
it bunged up the toilet
now the fats gone so bad
it's bunged up the drains
and it's started to rain
and outside the water is rising

It's all the fault of
the stuff that we do
the condoms, the wet wipes

we flushed down the loo
micro bead suds
and cotton wool buds
that have polluted the seas all around us

It's all the fault of
ill informed us
we were conned and were lied to
told "don't make a fuss"
companies guarded their profits
as they all picked our pockets
and still the water is rising

It's all the fault of
complacent man
someone will stop it
they'll do what they can
half the Earth is still burning
but we're still not learning
the clock on the wall now reads midnight.

Sometimes we have no idea if the news we are being fed is true or not. This is my take on fake news!

Fake News

Fake news
on the internet
Fake goods
inside the shops
Fake tan
on your bodies
The fakedom
never stops

Fake love
if you've got the money
Fake gold
if you've been conned
Fake empathy
from the D.S.S.
Fake warmth
if you get cold

Fake boobs
if you have operation
Fake cheeks
pump up your rump

Fake eyebrows
on your forehead
Fake hair
like Donald Trump

Fake money
in Monopoly
Fake sugar
if you're diabetic
Fake meat
if you've gone veggie
Fake rhymes
if you're poetic.

I wrote this in my hospital bed in the LGI whilst in bloody agony between morphine shots waiting for my broken hip to be replaced. It cheered me up a bit at the time.

Morphine

We're back on the morphine again
it kills all the anger
it kills all the pain
it numbs the agony
of broken bones
the only down side
is you can't take it home!

I'm not sure why this is called depression as its message
is pretty positive. It's a poem reminding us to cheer up,
get on with it and don't let life, and that black dog, get
you down.

Depression

Like a bar-b-que
in the pouring rain
you've got to keep
that flame alive

Like a leaf caught
in a howling gale
you're forced
to duck and dive

Just keep your home fire burning
from deep inside your gut
never let the light go out
or get stuck inside a rut

Never let that flying shit
collide with your personal fan
there's enough of it going around
to drown your fellow man

Never let that dog run free
don't let it bring you down
don't let its snapping jaws catch you
keep both feet on the ground

Life is for the living
there isn't any sequel
cos when it comes right down to it
all men are cremated equal.

2019 wasn't that great a year. As I write this 2020 is proving even worse. It seems to be a crap year for stuff happening, or not happening. This poem was inspired by a 1969 track by the genius that was Frank Zappa.

Trouble Everyday

I'm getting mighty pissed off
watching my TV
checking out the news
and all the crap I see
every single day
is just a fucking mess
and when it's going to change
is anybody's guess

The one thing that I say
it's just trouble everyday

From our local city council
to the Houses of Westminster
from everybody's brother
to everybody's sister
from VAR in football
to the English cricket team
from the speed of local broadband
life's a nightmare not a dream

The one thing that I say
it's just trouble everyday

We deserve a whole lot better
in this twenty first century
but war and strife's still ruling
it's just more obscenity
there's got to be a better world
we were promised jet packs
we were promised a better future
instead of fucking head wacks
that cause trouble everyday
I'm sick of trouble everyday

If you are a regular reader of my work, or if you've seen me live you've probably figured I don't like the Conservative Party and their policies. I really don't like this particular member.

Like a pubic hair on a toilet seat

Like a pubic hair on a toilet seat
you really piss me off
like a doctor in a hernia ward
you make me want to cough

Like a chameleon on a tartan rug
you never show true colours
like wrist watch on a businessman
you've got no time for others

like a violinist in a folk group
you're always on the fiddle
like a double ended yo-yo
you play both ends against the middle

Like the eyes of the executioner
peering from his mask
like a piece of spat out chewing gum
you're sticking to your task

Like a one legged man in an arse kicking race
you're next to fucking useless
like Sherlock Holmes in a Cluedo game
you're absolutely clueless

Like two lovers on a moonless night
you're groping in the dark
like Frankenstein's monster on the slab
you're missing a vital spark

Like a dyslexic agnostic
that doesn't believe in Dog
you're stuck in the wrong century
Cos you're Jacob William Rees Mogg

I dislike this particular member of the Conservative
Party even more.

Ian Duncan Fucking Smith

Ian Duncan Fucking Smith
has the shifty eyes
of a lunatic
failed his education
lied in his Who's Who
a nasty little specimen
inside the Tory zoo
made up official figures
to destroy the welfare state
An evil little paranoid man
whose heart is filled with hate
for Britain's sick and disabled
and them without a job
Ian Duncan Fucking Smith
writes them off as useless slobs
and no matter how sick you are
he forces you to work
and thinks behind every sick note
is someone who's a shirk
and now he's robbed our benefits
this despicable little man
has his greedy eyes on our futures

and intends to rob our pensions plan
he wants us to carry on working
until we're seventy five
all in the full knowledge
half of us won't be alive.
we'll all be bloody worked to death
casualties in his class war
Ian Duncan Fucking Smith
that right wing Tory whore.

To date I have never won the lottery. Am I twisted and bitter about it? Yes! You bet I am.

Luck

Jesus rides the dashboard
St Christopher's on my keys
St Michael's in my underpants
but my luck is on its knees

I have a lucky rabbit foot
that wasn't that good for the rabbit
I always keep my fingers crossed
bad luck is becoming a habit

I always wish on a full moon
and say hello to a passing Magpie
I always avoid hedgehogs after dark
and the jackdaws beady eye

My horoscope said don't trust the stars
but that all went over my head
my fortune cookie just lies in bits
it's a day to stay in bed

A black cat just shat on my mat
and sank its teeth in my bum
my dream catcher caught my nightmares
and left me feeling glum

My lucky dice is loaded
my crystal ball is cracked
my lucky charm is charmless
they shot the horse I backed

Your luck is what you make it
it could be good, it could be bad
but I've never won the lottery
and that's just fucking sad!

For the last couple or three years a very enterprising and jolly decent chappie called Mr. Jim has staged a small festival up on the moors above Scarborough. It's called Headland and I had a great time their last year and this really is poem to thank Jim and his many helpers for putting it on.

Headland

Friday lunchtime
is everything packed?
check out the weather
no need to take a mac

Road side – yellow sign
pointing up a track
turn left at a signed gate
find a spot and then unpack

Eventually your tents up
you head towards the action
a dragon on security
completes the checking in transaction

Stages are lit and songs are sung
great beers at three pound fifty
fruity flavoured ciders
to make your head go squiffy

The Crowbar sells their cocktails
there's pizza and fresh crepes
a decent cup of coffee
makes sure that you're awake

A postman is delivering
letters from woodland creatures
each child's eyes are open wide
and received with excited screeches

Three days and nights out in the sun
three days and nights of Headland fun
three days and nights in a tent of blue
three days and nights of portaloos

Now the tents are gone
the fields full of sheep
and the organiser and his team
have gone home to sleep

So thanks to everyone involved
to all who lent a hand
who made a magical Bank Holiday
at a festival called Headland

Back to my normal persona of being an angry old poet!

Two Fingers

Time to put two fingers up
to the ones who put us down
Time to put two fingers up
to the ones who make us frown
the Twitter trolls and on-line bullies
people who think Mrs. Brown is funny
ex-wives that stalk you on social media
people who fake their entries on Wikipedia
people who bump into you
when they're on their phone
people who just won't leave things alone
people who talk too loud on trains
people who act like they're bloody insane
people whose dogs shit in the street
people who think it's cool to cheat
people who are flash and show off all their wealth
people who moan about the state of their health
all the shit that's written in the Daily Fail
unsolicited stuff that's in the mail
people who don't mean what they say
loan sharks that lend, until pay day

Don't let their shit get under your skin
your better than that, now it's your turn to win
so don't let them mess inside your head
just keep on walking, keep looking straight ahead
dodge their bullets and keep good grace
wear that smile right across your face
don't feel bad if they all try to scoff
just raise two fingers and tell them to fuck off.

I did a few gigs with Ronnie Wray and his blues band.
Hence I tried to write a Yorkshire Blues poem. This is it.

A Blues Poem

There's blues inside a bottle
There's blues inside a song
There's blues on a football field
but that's Chelsea and that's wrong

There's blues my baby gave me
because she's gone away
There's blues about the weather
cos it's another crappy day

There's blues with Lightning Hopkins
with Blind Willie McTell
Old Whistling Jimmy Ramsbottom
that poor boy wasn't well

There's a bluesmen on the ocean
he's playing in the surf
but surf music just ain't the blues
cos he's turned out to be a smurf

And then there's Box Car Willie
a very frightening disease
and Wee Little Jimmy Ackroyd
who came up to just your knees

Peg Leg Clegg from Huddersfield
and that Morbid Sod from Hull
his blues were hypothermia
cos his heating all went wrong

So when you hear those blues songs
be happy, don't feel blue
cos there's always some poor bugger
that's a lot worse off than you!

Yet another moan about not winning the Lottery (am I fixated, perhaps I am!)

Lottery

Bloody hell another week
I haven't won the Lottery
it could be me, it could be you
it could be just a mockery
Euromillions and Thunderball
every week I win fuck all
I chose my numbers carefully
each one means a lot to me
the number of a previous house
the birthday of a divorced spouse
I think my chances are increased
by adding the number of the beast
the number of hits the Beatles had
divided by the age of my Dad
the number of times I brush my teeth
plus the witches on that blasted heath
fire burn and cauldron bubble
the Lottery's a load of troubled
if you forget to fill it in
that'll be the week you win!
and them that win and say their lives won't change
well I think they're just fucking deranged

And them that say they'll not stop working
their heads are wrong, they must be raving
if the Lottery millions drop on me
a cloud of dust is all you'll see
a sunshine beach and a glass of beer
chucking rocks at them that come near
but I haven't won and times are hard
give us a quid, for another scratchcard.

Written as a little challenge at the Headland Festival

Wasp

I'm a Wolverhampton Wanderer
in a Castleford Tigers shirt
I'll buzz around you secretly
then sting you where it hurts
I'll scatter all your picnics
play hell in your outdoor caff
I'll land on your cup of coffee
just to have a laugh
I'll break up any meeting
whether social or religious
just a little buzz from me
sends everybody witless
my cousins are protected
everyone loves bees
but out comes the rolled up newspaper
as soon as you see me
I'm the uninvited party guest
I made a nest on Jesus' cross
I'm the yellow and black terrorist
I'm the common garden wasp.

I like this poem a lot. I like music and, in my time I've
seen a lot of it. I also write books about witches and have
looked at some elements of black and white magic. This
poem is a combination of the two.

The Devils Rock & Roll

If you lose your woman
and you lose your soul
it don't mean a damn
it's just the devils rock and roll
if your winning lottery ticket
get's washed in your old jeans
and the bosses lay you off
cos they've brought in a machine
and everything you touch
seems to turn to shite
your days are numbered
and you don't sleep well at night
turn to the bottle to have a little tipple
when you realise your partner
has got that extra nipple
and your credit cards been nicked
and your pockets just been picked
that your cats got hooves
and it's worked out all your moves
there's a goat inside your wardrobe

and a succubus wears your bathrobe
and there's horns on the head
of the pizza delivery man
and you realise that Black Sabbath
isn't just a band
and you went to the crossroads
but you still can't play guitar
and although the tunes been lifted
you'll always bear the scar
and God proclaimed two Richards
to us he would bequeath
Jesus gave us Cliff, but the Devil gave us Keith
and there ain't a cobbler that can
fix the hole that's in your soul...
relax, sit back, and suck it up
It's just the devils rock and roll.

This poem is a sort of homage to the old fashioned
English seaside McGill postcard.

Sticky
Everyone loves a bit of sticky
everyone loves a bit of goo
cannabis oil and candy floss
Post-it notes and Irish stew

Postage stamps and melted tar
Marmite trickling down its jar
your underwear in this hot weather
Germans in their shorts of leather

A toffee crisp left in the sun
marmalade spread on a sticky bun
sticky fingers in the till
dog poo on an espadrille

Sello-tape and KY Jelly
barbeque Sauce spread on pork belly
sticky nose from sniffing glue
stick it to me I'll stick to you

But the greatest bit of sticky
the sticky that always shocks
is that little bit that oozes out -
From a stick of Scarborough rock.

Written the day the Conservative Party voted to put
Boris in charge. Looking back it could be prophetic.

PM
Like a vampire in a blood bank
you want to suck me dry
like a washing line on a windy day
you hang me out to dry
like a crazy back seat driver
you've got me round the bend
like a spate of criminality
you set out to offend
like the figure that stands behind me
when I look inside the mirror
you'll specify the fava beans
to eat with my cooked liver
like a ferret up my trouser leg
you're a pain my bloody knackers
you're like a cheap and nasty plastic toy
that fell out of a Christmas cracker
if I wanted to build an idiot
I'd ask to borrow your brain
I know I like a fucking joke
but this is just insane
a cockwombling Eton rich boy
who's a muppet, not a man
 Boris is our next PM
just watch the shit as it hits the fan.

I'm sure that as a race we're getting less and less intelligent. We might even be devolving. What's worse is that these days they seem to end up on TV.

Dickheads

There's dickheads in the government
dickhead's in the news
dickhead's writing articles
airing their dickhead views

There's dickhead's on the council
there's dickhead's owning shops
there's dickhead's on the internet
where dickheadery never stops

There's dickheads in the public houses
dickheads on the road
dickheads so full of self importance
you'd think their dickhead would explode

There's dickheads making movies
dickhead's at the zoo
I wouldn't trust a dickhead
to sit the right way on the loo

There's dickheads in the boardroom
screwing up our industry
seems there's more dickheads out there
than the likes of you and me

There's a training ground for dickheads
where they practice being senseless
wou can watch their antics every week
on Alan Sugar's "Apprentice"

I like word play and double meanings. This poem
celebrates them.

Boil In The Bag

Boil in the bag is not a cooking term
If you're a dermatologist

A bird in the hand means something else
if you're an ornithologist

Beating about the bush
is an S&M perversion

Arriving at the end of the line
means you've missed your bloody station

If you think that everything's coming your way
Then you're driving in the wrong lane

Experience is that wonderful thing
that makes you know you've screwed up again

A man's got do what a mans gotta do
and a woman does what he canna

Time files like an arrow
but fruit flies like a banana

Give them an inch and they'll take a mile
is the Ordinance Survey's job

Saying "he should be bloody well hung!"
don't mean he's gotta a big knob

If at first you don't succeed
then sky diving's not for you

The same old phrase can mean many things
just depends on your position

But "we're all in this together" shite
is just a lie when said by politicians!

I've no idea who or what the Fuckity Man is but I think he would make a great comic book character.

The Fuckity Man

Please don't mess
with the Fuckity Man
he'll screw you up
every way he can.
He's evil, he's vicious
he's nasty as well
he lives two doors down
from the gates of Hell.
He hides your keys
and sups your pint.
Scratches your car
and starts up fights
He gets the lemmings
to jump off cliffs.
He'll steal your stash
and smoke your spliffs.
Please don't mess
with the Fuckity Man
he'll steal your lover
and sleep with your mam.
He'll break your heart
and mess with your plans

He's the king of thieves
like a petulant panda
he eats shoots and leaves.
He's the living nightmare
that haunts your days.
He invented the fidget
and other daft crazes.
He's an evil fucker
and he don't give a damn.
So please don't mess
With the Fuckity Man

Photos of peoples food on social media drives me crazy.

Photography
There's tons of stuff to photograph
city streets or countryside.
Kitten playing with balls of string
and beaches at low tide.
Sunsets over mountains
dawn breaking out at sea.
Point your camera this way
and take a photograph of me.
Photographs of flowers.
Photographs of snow.
Photographs of rainy days,
and watching water flow.
Or wild life in its habitat,
or wild life in a zoo.
Photos nice and wholesome,
photos slightly blue.
Photos of people in the street,
or people at their work.
Performers singing songs for you,
Dancers as they twerk.
Pollution in the atmosphere,
plastic floating in the river.
So why the fuck you're filling Instagram
of photos of your dinner?

Yawn, yawn. I wrote this in exasperation with the prolonged Brexit fiasco.

Boredom

I'm bored with bloody Brexit
I'm bored with bloody news
I'm bored with reading papers
I've got the Brexit overkill blues
I'm bored with the latest exposé
of Donald Trump's new wig
I'm bored with vegan options
I don't give a flying fig
I'm bored with the latest X Factor
The Voice and Britain's Lack of Talent
manufactured entertainment
a replacement Valium habit
I'm bored with the latest shock reports
about Britain's sexual habits
I don't really give a shit
if you go home and bang like rabbits
I'm bored with Royal Princes'
and the antics of their wives
I want to scream at Hello Magazine
just get a fucking life!
I'm bored with hipster bearded men
in trendy coffee houses
I just want a cup of coffee

Not a ginger molasses latte
I'm bored with education
but that's just mortar board
I'm also very bored with Art
but that's just drawing board
I'm bored with television
I just don't really care
I'm bored with my own poetry
so let's just leave it there!

Again, another poem about aging. I think I'm developing a thing about it. However, it's also really a swipe at austerity and the Conservative Party.

I'm so old

I'm so old
I remember trams
I remember green gas lamps
and the tally man
who went by the name
of Septic Knuckles
in the streets where even
the rats had muscles
when Snickers Bars were
known as Marathons
where the only good Samaritan
is a bad Samaritan
and a dog with two ears
was a rarity
where everything had a price
and nothing came for free
apart from rickets
and scarlet fever
where even Jesus
was a disbeliever
there was nothing good
about the bad old days

and now I read a paper
and I fill with rage
cos Tory austerity
is dragging us back
sixty years of welfare state
is under attack
whilst the CEOS's
cheer the Fat Cat day
they've already earned
what we can in a year
It's enough to make
An old man cry
I don't know how to stop things
but by fuck we'll have to try.

These days I don't believe a thing a politician says. I don't believe half of what I read or what I hear. More fake news and hearsay.

Belief

You can't trust a politician
especially when it speaks
you can't trust 30 quid
to see you through the week
you can't trust Pennine Express
to run their trains on time
you can't trust the Government
not to pinch what's yours and mine
you can't trust the internet
whether true or if its false
you can't trust your bowel movements
that's why there's Epsom Salts
you can't trust the council
not to knock good buildings down
you can't trust the President
not to act like a fucking clown
you can't trust the Russians or the Chinese
you can't trust any take away
to cook a meal that's peanut free
so don't believe in what you hear
and only half of what you see

don't believe in prophecies
don't believe in me
don't believe in Fortune Cookies,
they're made in Rotherham
don't believe the Tories
their right is always wrong
the only thing to believe in
one thing that never fails
is that every fucking weekend
D.F.S will hold a sale.

A side swipe at what was becoming a British Institution.

No Idea What's Going On

I'm at a loss to work it out
what the fuck is going on?
The whole damn world has gone to shit
and everything's gone wrong

There's loonies in the Whitehouse
nutters in Whitehall
something's that used to mean something
now don't mean anything at all

Every days a puzzle
as to what will happen next
you couldn't write it if you tried
it's got us all perplexed

for the life of me I can't work out
just who is using who
I'm a little bit more older
and a fuck sight more confused

How can it still be going on
how is it that last summer
Channel Five began to screen
another series of Big Brother?

A poem about the destruction of our industries, the effects of the Conservatives austerity policies and their willing destruction of the welfare state.

When I was a kid,

I could have been a miner,
an engine driver,
a bloke that mended things
with a bloody great big spanner

I could have worked the docks
I could have worked in steel
I could have done a hundred things
to earn a damn good meal.

I could have worked on t'buses
I could have worked on trains,
I could have been in overalls
and fixed the broken drains

There were employment opportunities
there was never a need to rob
every town had its own industry
every town had its own jobs

But now we have the food banks
and they've cut away the dole
social security has gone
there's just a big black hole

So how do we earn a living
how do we earn our pay
everything we fought to gain
Westminster took away

The only thing that's left
is to work in iron and steel
my missus takes in ironing
And then goes out and steals.

A poem about defiance in the face of adversity

Too many zeros

Too many zeros
Not enough heroes
Everything's just so-so
The areas a no-go
Our lives a bloody side show
Controlled by fucking psychos
Scammed by all the wide boys
Time to put away the child's toys
To shout and make some loud noise
Write yourself some smart prose
Keep grinning till your smiles froze
Their uniforms are just clothes
Designed to beat you down
Now we're stuck with no hope
No money is a bad joke
Better score some strong dope
Better take a long toke
And smoke the sucker down
Only look out for the good times
Don't fall for all those hard lines
Watch out for all the bad signs

Of bodies drawn in outline
Weird scenes inside the gold mine
Thinking for yourself is no crime
Now everyone is sighing
Can't be bothered lying
The alcohol is flying
Can't be arsed with trying
In the midst of life we're dying

This one's for my father. It's about my memories of the
football games he took me to when I was a kid. The team
is the 1958 Leeds Utd. team. It's odd, but all my early
memories of Leeds seem to be in black and white.

This one's for Jackie Overfield

The sunsets in the background
behind the Lowfield stand.
Factory chimneys on horizons
when the fans all left by tram.
Tthe fifties when all our teams
played in black and white.
Homemade scarves and wooden rattles
in smoggy, gas-light nights.
The ghosts of players lost in time
echo round the final whistle.
Their game is done, their boots are hung
there's no one left to listen
to the names, the fans all chanted
the names from old team sheets.
Don Revie, Jimmy Ashall,
Grenville Hair and Georgie Meek,
Noel Payton, Billy Humphries,
Jackie Overfield and Chris Crowe.
Archie Gibson, Jackie Charlton,
and Ted Burgin in the goal.

Their names are carved on gravestones
Somewhere in this land
But their fame lives on forever
in hearts of old Leeds fans
whose lives too, soon will end,
when there'll be no one left to say
they were standing in the Scratching Shed
and saw Jackie Overfield play.

These days there's always some shit storm happening somewhere. Usually its caused by something that's got nothing to do with us, we just get caught in the crossfire. This is a warning to keep your head down.

Shit storm

There's a shit storm brewing
and it's heading straight for us
it's no use complaining
or kicking up a fuss

Better wear a helmet
get hold of an umbrella
better lock your doors at night
and hide inside the cellar

Better lay awake at night
better live in fear
there's things out there to get us
dangers always near

At least that's the opinion
promoted by our press
who print all sorts of bollocks
to keep us all suppressed

To keep us in a state of worry
to stop us asking why
to stop us working out the truths
behind the politicians lies

To never ask the question
that will lead to their disgrace
who started off this shit storm
in the first fucking place?

Here's a wry look at love, or where not to have sex.

Love

Love takes many forms
but never have sex on a bench
you get splinters in the back of your hand
when you pause to take a rest
and everyone starts looking
and offering advice
some of its quiet practical
but some's not very nice
and don't have sex in a taxi cab
they'll charge your double fare
and you'll stop to eat after sex on the beach
cos of all the sand which is there
and rule out sex on a golf course
there's eighteen holes you know
each one marked with a little flag
to show you where to go
and never have sex on a Double Decker
always go for a Mars Bar
cos a Mars a day helps you work rest and play
and that way you'll go far
and never have sex on an IKEA bed
or any flat-pack, self assembly
cos there's always a screw left over
and it ends up very trembley

Love takes many forms
it's what makes the world go round
and no matter what the cynics say
there's enough to go around
so make love whilst you can
it's better than making war
but for all our sakes don't be like that couple last night
please wait till you get home.

I wrote this after reading about how all our on-line data being harvested by someone and sold off to someone else.

Data

Where's my bloody data gone
someone's sold it off
now Mark Zuchenburg knows
every time I have a cough
every cookies loaded
to pinch the details of your life
they'll even send it back to you
with suggestions for a wife.
every time we surf the web
or watch catch up TV
there's a little data package
looking in on you and me

Where's me bloody data gone
someone's sold it on
to help form public opinion
and no one thought it wrong
to help persuade us how to vote
and feed us with false news
to fall victim to that click bait
designed to change our views

someone's pinched our data
and seen our private stuff
they've looked at all our photos
they just can't get enough
and now I'm really worrying
it was those photos of my arse
that persuaded all America
to put Donald Trump in charge

A poem about Viagra – not a lot else to say.

What's the story

What's the story
morning glory
leapt out of bed
leeling horny

Fumbled and tumbled
and fell down the stairs
and tried to have sex
with everything there

He rogered the Rabbit
had a go at the cat
the dog had to growl
and hid under the mat

He's ready for anything
animals, women and men
Got his vitamins mixed up with
Viagra again!

The opening phrase came to me one day and I thought it funny. It took a while but I got a poem out of it. It's been in my live act for ages. One night as I was walking home from a gig through a deserted Scarborough town centre, a voice echoed down the street. It simply said "Oi poet – Never put your willie in a deep fat fryer." It's nice to know people have taken my advice.

Poetic Advice

Never put your willie in a deep fat fryer.
Never poke a monkey with a stick.
Never let a weasel up your trouser leg.
Never grab a parrot by its dick.
Never trust authority.
Never trust your nose.
Always duck and dive
and keep nimble on your toes.
Always wash your hands at night
and always say a prayer.
Always remember germs and Jesus
are everywhere.
Never trust the papers
they treat us like blind mice.
Never trust a drunken poet
to give you good advice.
You may think I'm talking shite
but I promise I'm no liar.
Trust me – Never put your willie in a deep fat fryer.

I use to like Richard Branson & Virgin. They had great record shops and I thought they were on our side. Now as a huge mega company, they are asking the Government to bail out their railways and their airline, and they sued the NHS, now I've no respect for them anymore.

Virgin on the ridiculous

It's all gone bloody silly
bordering on daft
what do you think you are doing?
you having a fucking laugh?
you're beginning to take the piss mate
you're pulling on my leg
you're pulling on my plonker
you're messing up my head
you've started taking liberties
you're getting on my wick
we used to have respect for you
but now you're acting like a prick
 you've spoilt your reputation
you've gone and marked your card
you're off your bloody rocker mate
you're out your tiny mind
you're living in a fantasy
stuck in your own dream

Your attitudes and platitudes
just make me want to scream
how come they think you're qualified
to make trains all run on time
you dropped a mighty bollock
on that Virgin, East Coast Mainline
so come on Richard Branson
with your hidden, off- shore wealth
show you care, sell off your shares
and stop fucking up our National Health

It doesn't matter if it's Virgin or any other company, the privatisation of the railways hasn't worked. Somehow in the board rooms of the companies that run them, they seem to have forgotten how to run passenger services.

East Coast Main Line

People in trains
with loud headphones
using their mobiles
In the quiet zone

Blocking the aisles
With Samsonite cases
Drunks having arguments
Coming back from the races

Toilets that block
And toilets that roll
Don't flush in the station
Cos it's just a big hole

Dumping more shit
On the East Coast Main Line
Where sometimes they manage
to run trains on time

Wi-Fi that drops
in all the wrong places
the doom and the gloom
on travelers faces

Incoherent announcements
No one can hear
Let the train take the strain
But it's just too fucking dear

We've all been here. A few drinks and a stop-off on the way home via the pizza place or the burger kebab wagon that sells the take-away food that only tastes food when you're pissed.

The Alcoholic Munchies

Pukka Pies and a diner kebab
chips with peas and gravy
instant pleasure to satisfy
that alcoholic craving

After 4 or 5 pints of bitter
you really need to eat
any food you can find on sale
after midnight on the street

Cholesterol fried in batter
garlic sauce on fish and chips
bollocks to the extra inches
gathering on your hips

A Big Mac or a KFC
with corn and extra gravy
never seems to satisfy
that alcoholic craving

You never know just what you want
but you know you want it now
it doesn't really matter
if It's sheep or pork or cow

But as you close your eyes to sleep
remember the words of your mother
it's the devils own job to scrape stale kebab
with chili sauce, off a duvet cover.

A poem that's just riffs on the word "line".

Lines
There's deadlines
Headlines
Lines of coke and speed
Train lines
Help lines
Blood lines when you breed

Straight lines
Parallel lines
Lines underneath your eyes
Telephone lines
Tube lines
Lines to score a try

Hem lines
Jaw lines
Lines in every song
Guide lines
Hard lines
When everything goes wrong

This is just a list of words
that all end with a line
I thought I'd make a poem of them -
What a fucking waste of time!

There's a bit of the sea near Scarborough that's dead.
The story was told me by a surfer friend – this is for him.

Surfers Poem
There's poison floating out at sea
it's killing the sea bed
industrial pollution
is giving fish two heads

Every surfer takes a risk
on every wave they ride
bacteria and micro beads
washed up on every tide

Every bather takes a risk
from the shit that's in the foam
your toes will rot and then drop off
you're better off at home

Fish and chips and candy floss
sun and sand but no blue flags
outlets and rock pools all
jammed up with plastic bags

The seaweed's gone the sea is dead
there's no more fishing trips
what a fucking price to pay
for a bag of oven chips.

A poem about slippy things. Ironically a short while after writing it I slipped, fell over and broke my hip. Hey ho that's karma for you.

Slippy

Mud is pretty slippy
eels are slippery too
seaweed on the rocks is slippy
be careful lest you fall

Winter ice is dangerous
wet floors and yellow signs
just caught fish and oil for chips
we live in slippery times

Jellyfish are slippery
cos they haven't got a spine
fallen leaves in puddles
will get you every time

Jelly's pretty slippery
so's fresh dog poo on the street
all sorts of things are slippery
to knock us off our feet

Sex is pretty slippery
if you do it right
slipping and a sliding
rumpy pumpy in the night

All sorts of stuff is slippery
to send us on our bums
but there's nothing quiet as slippery
as a politicians tongue!

Sometimes I feel that the people in power just can't be human. The title is "borrowed"from a track by Country Joe MacDonald. I like Country Joe.

Zombies in the house of madness

There's vampires sitting in Whitehall
werewolves in the House of Lords
goblins and lesser demons
in charge of our town halls

There's blood sucking giant leeches
in charge of all our banks
our lives are all decided
by creatures thick as planks

Two faced weasels in the city
screwing me and you
snakes control our media
that filter all our news

There's zombies in the house of madness
that drive us up the wall
but that orange clown in the Whitehouse
just fucking Trumps them all.

I wrote this poem one night, after seeing a bloke fall off his chair, despite being warned not to lean back. It was in The Merchant pub, the Fuzz Junkies were playing. I like the Fuzz Junkies.

Sometimes when you live on the edge

Sometimes when you live on the edge
it's easy to fall off
Sometimes it's hard to tell if you need
a shit or a shave or a cough

Sometimes what you want
is never what you need
Sometimes the only answer
is a bloody great bag of weed

Sometimes you're better off
going out and getting pissed
Whatever your philosophy
life's always hit and miss

Nostalgia ain't what it used to be
the futures looking risky
better live for now, get another drink
and make it double whiskey

So don't bother looking forward
try never to look back
shove all your broken dreams
back in the refuse sack

Go to the bar, have another drink
you know it's what you need
and keep your fingers tightly crossed
for that bloody great bag of weed.

I've been heckled more than once. This is for them.

Hecklers and talkers

Hecklers and talkers
the curse of open mics
we'd like to say to all of them
that it's you we really like.
You make our life so challenging
to help us learn our acts
we love to hear your chit chat
we love playing to your backs
and watching as you use your phone
sending selfie's home
I'm sure the world won't miss you
if you leave Facebook alone.
How would you like it
if I turned up at your work
and talked and yelled and shouted
and acted like a jerk?
You've beer to drink and songs to hear
whilst we try to entertain
and if you don't like it go outside
have a fag - don't be such a pain.
So thank you for your tolerance
thanks for your attention
you never thought that after all
you buggers finally got a mention.

A poem that's simply a series of unanswered questions.

Deep Shit

Why are we always in deep shit?
Why is our shit never shallow?
Why is it our paths always twisted
and never the straight and the narrow?

Why do we have an election
when the Government always gets in?
Why do we play t'National Lottery
when there's never a chance we can win?

Why isn't there mouse flavoured cat food?
Why nail down the lid on a coffin?
How does the bloke in charge of the snow plough
get to his work in t'morning?

Why, when you order a pizza
does it come in a box that is square?
What happens when dry ice is melted?
And why is a boxing ring square?

Why, when things get shitty
do we always blame it on fate?
You always complained I came early
but it was you that always came late!

How can choirs all sing like angles
when the devil has all the best tunes?
How come there's always a bloody great prick
that turns up just to burst our balloons?

But why bother looking for answers
curiosity once killed our cat.
The less that we know the better we sleep,
and our Government likes it like that.

Out of all the poems I do in my live act this is by far and away the one that audiences like the most. It's stood me in good stead for the last four or five years. I wrote in one go, in a fit of pique after being unfriended, not a word has since been changed.

Facebook Poem

I've just been un-friended on Facebook
Does it look like that I give a shit?
Thank God that you'll no longer share with me
your thoughts and your wisdom and wit

No longer will I have to put up with
your opinions and photos of life.
Your comical cats and photos of twats
that you met when you're out with your wife

I've just been un-friended on Facebook
hip- hip- hip bloody hurray.
No more dubious comments on Brexit
and your fetish about Theresa May.

No more misguided missives from fascists.
Jokes that are sexist and fail.
Your comments on everyday living
taken from t' Telegraph, Sun and The Mail

I've just been un-friended on Facebook,
now I'm liberated, cleansed and feel free
from all of your dubious comments
why the fuck did you send them to me?

Now you can carry on living
your day-to-day life in your way
and I'll get on doing whatever I do
not caring what your Facebook might say.

I've just been un-friended on Facebook
I assume that you now wish me ill luck
but I'm sorry to say I've have a great day
and frankly, I don't give a fuck!

Scarborough Council were determined to pull this old,
iconic and much loved building down. Cultural vandals.
To this day where it once stood it's still an empty site, a
great Conservative Party legacy to our town.

The Futurist

Everybody knows
our councils got no brains.
Everybody knows
they can't even sort out drains

Everybody knows
they're not philanthropists
but what the fuck they're doing
pulling down the Futurist

Flamingoland's paid thousands
into Scarborough Tory coffers
maybe to make sure
there are no other offers

Conservation, preservation
and heritage go west
just so our local councilors
can feather a secret nest.

We lost the Flora Gardens
The Opera House and more
Tourist Information centers
closed down for evermore

They're pulling down our town
and selling off the ground
it'll only cost 4 million quid
to knock the Futurist down

Cultural vandals in
the corridors of power.
If the buggers were in Blackpool
they'd be selling off the Tower.

No matter how loud we shout
the Council still won't listen
our opinions don't matter
they ignored the signed petition

Corruption in the Council
that's not for me to say
but the message from the people is
"We want the Futurist to stay!"

Written just after my 2017 heart attack this is a result of watching just how hard our nurses and doctors work and just how bloody precious our NHS is. It's dedicated to them and the people who came to visit me in the cardiac unit. For people outside Scarborough the Harbour Bar is the 1950's ice cream salon on the seafront.

Happiness

Happiness comes with
a Whisper Bar
or a knickerbocker glory
in the Harbour Bar

An unexpected orgasm
or a tax rebate
paying off your debts
wiping clean the slate

Happiness comes
with a new CD
discovering you haven't got
an STD

Finding a tenner
in an old jacket pocket
lighting up a joint
that takes off like a rocket

Happiness comes
with a living wage
food in your stomach
and a pension in old age

A society that cares
for its ill and sick
and not been sold
to money grabbing pricks

who starve it of cash
to make sure it fails
so say it loud - say it proud
our National Health is not for sale.

This poem was a birthday poem written for Luke
Pearson who is one of the finest white soul singers I've
ever seen.

Soul Man

The soul man sings his songs tonight
in the midnight hour, it's a rappers delight
Pattie La Belle and Major Lance
The Isley Brothers - Do you wanna dance?
Fontella Bass and Curtis Mayfield
The one and only Dusty Springfield
The Righteous Brothers and Pointer Sisters
Rufus Thomas and the Whispers
Belting out that Northern Soul
Teddy Prendergast stands by the door
Harold Melvyn and his Bluenotes
if it's sweet soul music that floats your boat
get you down to Robin Hoods Bay
the soul mans singing Marvin Gaye.
A dose of soul can cure all ills
check out Aretha Franklin and Tammy Terrell.
A dose of soul can cure all wrongs
So Happy Birthday Luke! Now sing your song!

A poem written about funny noises in the night. Of course it's just the house settling, but settling what?

Footsteps

There's footsteps
in the corridor
footsteps up the stairs
footsteps on the floor above
they catch you unawares
they echo when you're all alone
they rattle in the night
in the silence they get nearer
as you hair stands up in fright.
The footsteps in the corridor
of people long time dead
of people who lived this life before
of people who died inside their bed
people killed in two world wars
as bombs came raining down
people who died of illness
 as diseases spread around.
People good, people bad,
people happy, people sad
people who had money
people who were poor
at night the footsteps echo
of them that lived before.

Monologues

For years I have enjoyed and been influenced by monologues. The sort of material that Stanley Holloway recorded and performed, stuff like "Albert and The Lion". In my opinion the greatest monologue writer of them all was Marriott Edgar. In addition to being a pantomime dame he was also the writer that created the famous "Albert Ramsbottom" series for Stanley Holloway, and also created the wonderful historical based monologues about "The Battle of Hastings" and "The Magna Carta".

So here goes, this is a section of ,my own monologues. If by any chance after reading this section you find yourself wanting more, try to get hold of a book called "The Stanley Holloway Monologues" - it has some crackers in it.

The Legend of Robin Hood & Little John

When Robin Hood met Little John
he didn't have his trousers on.
Said Robin Hood to Little John
"Your quarter staff looks over long
It's more a half staff I would say."
Little John blushed & said "Look away.
It's been this long since I was eight
and although most people thinks it's great
being this big don't make you bold
you're more susceptible to colds
and living in a bloody wood
don't make the situation good.
Them draughts that whistle through the trees
freezes bits between the knees."
Said Robin Hood to Little John
"Why don't you put your trousers on?"
Said Little John to Robin Hood
"I really, really wish that I could,
cos striding through a patch of nettles
 is enough to test a brave man's mettle.
But very sadly my pants were pinched
by a Sherriff's man known as Vince.
He took them with him into town

and wants to charge me a full crown
before he'll return my pants to me."
and Robin Hood said "Right let's see."
So they walked that day to Nottingham
But when they saw he'd no trousers on
They arrested poor old Little John
It seems the sight caused great offence
My that Mi Lord is the case for the defense.

Drakes Bowls

He were playing at bowls down in Plymouth
an away game in the Middleton Cup
when someone ran up, and said best hurry oop
the Spanish Armadas turned up.

"They'll just have to wait," Said the Captain
as he took careful aim at the Jack
"This greens booked by me, I've got it till three
Tell 'em they'll have to come back."

"I'm not sure they're here for the bowling
They're in ships full of cannons and guns."
He pointed to sea and got hit on the knee
as Drake swapped his bowls for a drum

Then, as if to prove the man's story
the flash of a cannon they all seen
and a great cannon ball, passed over them all
and landed in middle of t'green.

It was one of the finest addresses
the bowlers of England had seen.
It knocked back the Jack, sent Drakes bowls right back
When they found them, they were on the next green

"Well that's a bit of a bugger!"
The judges said shaking their heads
But Drake beat his drum, and broke out the rum
And got everyone out of their beds.

By the time the English fleet hit the Channel
The Spanish had all buggered off
They'd all turned away, and sailed to Calais
And were shopping in Duty Free Shop.

Now this left old Drake with a problem
The Spanish had won the bowls game
so he put cup on a ship, then set fire to it
and straight for the Spanish he aimed

Then there followed a battle.
It ranged up and down on the sea.
When the smoke finally cleared, he singed off the beard
Of the Spanish, by ten games to three.

So Drake was proclaimed "Nation Hero"
and bowls gained National fame
But no matter how much history hypes it
bowls is still such a tedious game.

141

Vincent Van Gogh

Vincent van Gogh was a painter.
He painted the landscapes in France.
But a little known fact about Vincent
was he really enjoyed a good dance

He's dance in the local French cafes.
He dance through the night till the morn.
Then he'd go home by bus pick up a brush
and knock off a landscape by dawn.

One day whilst pissed on his absinthe
He tried painting whilst dancing a conga,
but whilst dancing a jig the art got too big
cos Absinthe makes the art grow longer.

But then he developed an earache
caused by the loud disco beat.
Though the act cost him dear, he cut off his ear
and frightened the dogs in the street.

He carefully wrapped it in paper.
To his mistress he sent it by post.
She wasn't impressed and ripped up his vest,
a sign their engagement was toast.

Now Vincent was deaf and heartbroken.
His dancing days now sadly finished.
He hadn't an ear for the music,
though his painting was never diminished.

The Man with the Detachable Dick

No one knew where he came from
they just knew that he made them all sick.
He was the man with no name, the man with no shame
the man with the detachable dick

He'd carry it round in his pocket
place it on mantelpiece, bookcase or shelf
But he never went far without a glass jar
cos to lose it was bad for his health

His lady friend liked his attachment.
She could have sex without his consent.
To save him the trouble she pushed in double,
and instead of coming she went.

Travelling was always a problem,
he caused a whole heap of fuss.
Complaints fair rained down, when he went off to town
and left it on number 9 bus.

The bus company tried to sue him
they didn't approve of his sort.
But their lawyer said no, the case wouldn't go
it would never stand up in the court.

He went through his life with his willie
until that unfortunate day,
he was limp wristed and got the thread twisted,
it fell off and got flushed away.

So if you travel right down to the seaside
where the effluent bobs on the beach
there's a dejected man holding a can
rubber gloves and a bottle of bleach

So consider you're lucky you fellers.
No matter how big or how small,
don't be daft, don't be silly, be proud of your willie,
cos its better than nothing at all.

Boudicca and the Romans

The Romans had landed in Briton
and building aqueducts, villas and roads.
They were doing quite well with the conquering
the poor Britain's who only wore woad.

Then they came to the boundaries of Yorkshire
where the Icini ruled as top tribe.
They were led by a Queen called Boudicca
that the Romans thought they could bribe.

So they sent her some wine in amphorae,
roast dormice in sesame seeds.
But the Icini were brought up on black pudding
served with tatties and turnips and mead

They looked at the Roman food parcel
and poked it with swords and with spears.
Then Boudicca stood tall, and said to them all
"You're not building roads around here!"

Now the Romans were working to contract
And were already late in their deeds

T

hey'd got lost in a bog down in Thetford
and fell in the river in Leeds

Building roads in straight lines proved a problem
in a country full of grey clouds and mist,
where no one could see the horizon
and it were proving a bit hit and miss.

So they sat down and came to agreement
to save bloodshed and more double pay
t'Romans stopped at Boudicca's boundary
waved their Eagles, then just walked away.

And that why if you go into Yorkshire
the roads are all bent, twisted and poor
and why it takes hours to travel
the length of the A64.

Shipping forecast

"And now the Shipping Forecast, issued by the Met
Office on behalf of the Maritime and Coastguard Agency
at 12:00am today."

Faroe, Fair Isle, Cromarty
Pullovers turning to cardigans
Jumpers for goalposts
On yer head – goal!

North Uster, South Uster, West Uster & East Finchley
Loony's on the bus
– not so good,
probably very bad.

Forth, Viking, Forties,
 Wet, Wet, Wet –
Love Is All Around
Definitely not so good – turning off.

Fisher, Dogger and Tyne
Visibility dropping
The fog on the Tyne is all mine, all mine,
The fog on the Tyne is all mine

Fisher and the German Bite
is a lot worse than it's Bach
Bad joke – strong winds,
Much flatulence

Humber, Thames and Dover
Visibility Black
Wibbly wobbly's aboard
Better not to go out - ever

Wight, Portland, Plymouth
Weasels running amok
slight precipitation,
always wear bicycle clips when mowing the lawn

Fitzroy, Biscay, Trafalgar
Light rain
A half nelson
Is better than no Nelson

Lundy, Sole and Farage –
Dicks always hang to the right
Low humidity
Fucking mad

Sole, Fastnet, Lundy
Ian Duncan Smith,
receding horizon
Even madder

Shannon, Rockall, Malin
Low mist - Hurricane Higgins
Typhoon Tyson
Baby please don't go

The Irish Sea, Hebrides, Crosby Stills Nash and Young
Marrakesh Express
Hippy shit –
Be sure to wear some flowers in your hair

South East Iceland
Frosty the snowman, thundery showers.
Moderate, never good,
occasionally bloody awful.

General Synopsis
Rain, then squally showers and, more rain.
Poor, becoming grim
Life sucks - Get a fucking helmet
The End.

The Tale of Lady Godiva

A Right Honourable Lady from Coventry
only had one decent dress.
It hung in her cupboard
and became all discoloured
till it looked an unholy mess.

So she sent this fine dress to the cleaners
to get it spruced up for a do
but it was so covered in muck
that the cleaners screwed up
and a dress that was yellow turned blue

So she went off to town to see t'cleaners
to make a complaint and a fuss
but she had now't to wear
so she let down her hair
and set off to catch the next bus.

But the driver was not that forthcoming
"You can't get on wearing just hair.
You're meant to be clad
the company will go mad.
Come back when you've something to wear."

So she called on a passing milkman
jumped on his horse and set off.
On her way into town
she made a few crowns
selling pintas at two pennies off

She sent to the town a strict message.
Told them that when she rides by
if anyone looked
she get a big hook
and poke out the offender's right eye

But one little bugger never heard it,
he was wearing his headphones at t'time.
When he stopped in the street
The Lady to greet
not knowing that it was a crime

He looked up just as she passed him,
and then a cruel wind it did blow.
It exposed her tits
and her ladyship's bits
that only her husband should know.

She screamed a scream so loudly
it frightened the horse out of its wits.
It set off at great speed,
no orders it'd heed
and was last seen on M26.

And that was the last anyone saw her.
There were reports from all over the place.
But she never returned
all entreaties she spurned.
She was ashamed at losing her face

And so in a charity shop window
sits a dress that is pretty and blue.
It's such a nice gown
on sale for a crown
but no one is forming a queue.

So heed this sad tale and take warning
Whenever you venture to town
Don't bother with hair.
Always wear underwear
Whether it's white or it's brown

Jack the Kipper

He was the champion fish gutter of Grimsby.
He went by the name Jack the Kipper.
He had a way with handling fish
ever since he was just a young nipper

He could fillet a flat fish in ten seconds flat
Halibut took a bit longer
but his fate it was sealed when he tackled an eel
of that particular type called a Conger

It slithered and slathered and turned on its tail.
It wriggled, it squirmed and fought back,
till it fastened its teeth on the bits underneath
the fish gutters bright yellow mac

His scream could be heard cross the Humber.
It frightened the seagulls in town.
It gave them the fits and an attack of the shits,
now the whole town is just white and brown

When he finally left the infirmary
he walked with a limp and a wince
being bit by a conger don't make it much longer.
In fact Jack lost the best part of an inch.

So Jack had to give up his gutting
In Grimsby he's now persona non grata
Despite still being nippy, he got sacked by the chippy
cos his sausage is now chipolata.

Peg Legged Dave the Pirate

In the days of the old wooden galleons
when bold pirates ruled the waves
a man made his fortune by sailing the ocean
and his name it was Peg Legged Dave

He sailed under t' skull and cross bones
on a ship called The Gilded Pig
With a parrot on both of his shoulders
and a hole in the top of his wig

He was famous from Filey to Flamborough
From Whitby to Robin Hoods Bay
For whetting his whistle, and flashing his mizzen
ahowing his bum, and then sailing away

He'd rob any ship he could capture
Taking silk, and French wine, and some grog
He'd pinch owt he could lay hands on
Owt that he thought he could flog.

He'd pinch brandy and rum and tobacco
He pinched timber and sugar in sacks

He even pinched some of his crews bottoms
And sulked when they asked for them back

One day he attacked a trader
that dealt in rare birds and livestock
he found crates of pigeons and an odd widgeon
two pelicans and a peacock

His end is was strange and mysterious
they say he fell foul of ship wreckers.
His ship sailed away and never seen to this day
cos his parrots were crossed with woodpeckers.

The Unfortunate Death of King Harold.

He's seen off the Vikings at Stamford Bridge
and was putting his feet up in York
when Harold read in the newspaper
some news that gave him a shock.

The Normans had landed in Hastings
and were expecting a bit of a scrap.
So he rubbed on his ear, and knocked back his beer
and quickly consulted his map.

When he eventually found Hastings
he realised it were on the South Coast
he had little time, and were cutting it fine
if he were to answer the Normans with force.

He ordered his generals to fix it
to get tickets on East Coast Main Line
but their web site was down, and he learnt with a frown
first train wasn't till eighteen sixty nine

The bus replacement service was knackered,
Mega Bus fully booked up.
So he called on his troops to pull on their boots
they'd walk - and they'd best hurry oop.

They fell into a bog in Northampton.
Fell foul of the by-pass in Staines.
They walked round and round, in Harlow New Town
and then it started to rain.

By the time they arrived down in Hastings
they were knackered, disheveled and wet.
They'd all had their fill, so they sat on a hill
whilst the Normans had hardly broke sweat.

"I've just walked the length of the country"
Harold complained to the ref.
But the ref wouldn't listen and blew on his whistle
and claimed that the noise made him deaf.

And then as a great battle happened
Harold swore and then swore a bit more.
When they cut out the chatter they learnt that the matter
he'd left his sword back in York, on t' pub floor

Now whilst the Normans were waiting for Harold
they'd discovered a good local pub.
They didn't sell wine, but they had a good time
playing darts with sharp pieces of wood.

One bloke was aiming for double,
a treble and then he would win.
But his arm it did tire, and it bounced off the wire
and headed towards top of t' hill.

Before anyone shouted a warning
it hit Harold straight in the eye.
He gave an odd blink, and started to sink
off his horse and then he expired.

When everyone saw what had happened
it broke all of the English troops hearts,
and they allowed the Normans to rule them
just as long as they never played darts.

And that's why if you go cross the Channel
you'll find rugby and football and boules.
But in all the French parts, you'll never find darts
Cos the buggers don't play by the rules.

Epilogue

So here we are at the end of my second book of poetry. It's been an absolute pleasure in putting it together. It was a huge surprise realising I had written so much. There again, performing live is a great impetus for writing more. Now heres a funny thingh, for some reason the many singer songwriters and bands I come across and perform with perform the same material time after time, and the audience dig it, and life goes on. I get up to shouts of "Have you got any new stuff?" Which leaves me wondering why singer songwriters can get away with old stuff but us poets are expected to come up with new stuff on a weekly basis. Is it that we're expected to react to events happening around us as if we are recorders of our time?

I'm writing this in May 2020, in the middle of the Covid-19 pandemic. Today is my fifty-fifth day of self isolation and, with the exception of walks to exercise the new hip, it's been the Covid-19 lock in. There are some poems in the book that reflect that. Today it's just been announced that gigs probably won't happen at all this year. It's a shame. I miss all my audiences from Scarborough to Leeds and beyond.

However I believe in new opportunities and I do believe that the internet is where we must look. At recent "We Shall Overcome" charity gig I performed to more people on the webcast that I could perform in front of in a year. I have also been performing three poems a day on my Graham Rhodes Performance Poet Facebook page and again more peole have been watching them per day than I could play to in a month. I've also been adding them onto my YouTube Channel. You can find them both on these links –

https://www.facebook.com/grhodesperformancepoet/
https://www.youtube.com/feed/my_videos

So that's it, until we can all meet again, please take care and keep safe.

Graham Rhodes –
Scarborough 2020

About the author

Graham Rhodes has over 40 years experience in writing scripts, plays, books, articles, and creative outlines. He has created concepts and scripts for broadcast television, audio-visual presentations, computer games, film & video productions, web sites, audio-tape, interactive laser-disc, CD-ROM, animations, conferences, multi-media presentations and theatres. He has created specialised scripts for major corporate clients such as Coca-Cola, British Aerospace, British Rail, The Co-operative Bank, Bass, Yorkshire Water, York City Council, Provident Finance, Yorkshire Forward, among many others. His knowledge of history helped in the creation of heritage based programs seen in museums and visitor centres throughout the country. They include The Merseyside Museum, The Jorvik Viking Centre, The Scottish Museum of Antiquities, & The Bar Convent Museum of Church History. He has written scripts for two broadcast television documentaries, a Yorkshire Television religious series and a Beatrix potter Documentary for Chameleon Films and has written three film scripts, The Rebel Buccaneer, William and Harold 1066, and Rescue (A story of the Whitby Lifeboat) all currently looking for an interested party.

His stage plays have performed in small venues and pubs throughout Yorkshire. "Rambling Boy" was staged at Newcastle's Live Theatre in 2003, starring Newcastle musician Martin Stephenson, whilst "Chasing the Hard-Backed, Black Beetle" won the best drama award at the Northern Stage of the All England Theatre Festival and was performed at the Ilkley Literature Festival. Other work has received staged readings at The West Yorkshire Playhouse, been shortlisted at the Drama Association of Wales, and at the Liverpool Lesbian and Gay Film Festival.

He also wrote dialogue and story lines for THQ, one of America's biggest games companies, for "X-Beyond the Frontier" and "Yager" both winners of European Game of the Year Awards, and wrote the dialogue for Alan Hanson's Football Game (Codemasters) and many others. You can find out more at his website http://www.grahamrhodes.com

Other books by Graham Rhodes

Available via Amazon
https://www.amazon.co.uk/-/e/B00JHIW2BQ

"Footprints in the Mud of Time,
The Alternative Story of York"

"The Jazz Detective."
(a detective story set in 1950's Soho)

The Agnes the Witch Series

"A Witch, Her Cat and a Pirate."

"A Witch, Her Cat and the Ship Wreckers."

"A Witch, Her Cat and the Demon Dogs."

"A Witch, Her Cat and a Viking Hoard."

 "A Witch, her Cat and TheWhistler."

"A Witch, her Cat and The Vampires."

"A Witch her Cat and the Moon People."

"A Witch Her Cat and a Fire Demon."

"A Witch her Cat and a Revolution."

166

"The York Sketch Book."
(a book of his drawings) – Out of Print

Photographic Books

"A Visual History of York."

"Leeds Visible History."

"Harbourside - Scarborough Harbour"
(A book of photographs available via Blurb)

"Lost Bicycles"
(A book of photographs of deserted and lost bicycles
available via Blurb)

"Trains of the North Yorkshire Moors"
(A Book of photographs of the engines of the NYMR
available via Blurb)

Printed in Great Britain
by Amazon

22577023R00098